VOGGY's
Recorder Book

This is my book:

....

Conception and manuscript: Martina Holtz
Compositions (P. 24, 27, 30, 31, 35, 40, 45, 50, 53, 54, 57, 91, 101, 104): Martina Holtz
Lyrics (P. 34, 38, 66, 69, 70, 81, 106): Martina Holtz

Cover design and illustrations: OZ, Essen (Katrin & Christian Brackmann)

© 2003 Voggenreiter Publishers
Viktoriastr. 25, D-53173 Bonn/Germany
www.voggenreiter.de
info@voggenreiter.de

ISBN: 3-8024-0464-5

Hello!

Welcome to my music tutorial for recorder!

With me as your tutor you can teach yourself to play
the recorder. I'll tell you all the things you need to
know. You don't need to be able to read music – I'll
also explain this to you as we go along, but it's still a
good idea to start learning the recorder with a teacher.
Perhaps your parents play the recorder a little and can help you if necessary.

I hope you have lots of fun with this book and your recorder. Good luck for your
musical future.

Voggy

Contents

Your Recorder

Before you start playing, I want to tell you a little bit about your recorder, which is a very old instrument that has been played for hundreds of years.

The recorder belongs to the family of **woodwind instruments** (because it is made of wood and is blown). There are many types of recorder in different sizes and pitches. When people speak of a recorder, they usually mean a **soprano recorder** (or **descant recorder** in the U.K.) because that is the one that is used most often. Nowadays, recorders are made of either wood or plastic. The choice of material depends on the sound (and your own taste).

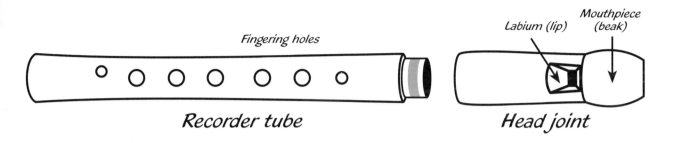

Fingering holes

Recorder tube

Labium (lip)

Mouthpiece (beak)

Head joint

This is what your recorder looks like. Be careful not to poke your finger into the labium because its inside edges are very sensitive.

Larger recorders often comprise three parts, with a detachable foot joint. Many recorders have double holes for the lower notes, because they allow some notes to be played better and with a much nicer tone.

The Correct Position

When playing the recorder it is very important to relax your body.

- *Your back should be as straight as possible and your head inclined slightly, but still held upright.*

- *Shoulders, arms, hands and fingers should be as relaxed as possible.*

Finger Positions

Hold the recorder in both hands.
- The thumb of your **right** hand supports the recorder from below.
- Thumb and middle finger of your **left** hand balance the recorder.

Here are some examples showing how to hold the recorder correctly and incorrectly:

Wrong
The fingers are cramped.

Wrong
The fingers in the air are stretched out too far.

Right
The fingers are relaxed.

Starting off

Rest the **beak** (the uppermost part of the mouthpiece) on your lower lip, but don't let your teeth touch the mouthpiece.

Close your upper lip gently around the top edge of the beak. Make sure that no air escapes from the side of the recorder (e.g. from the corners of your mouth).

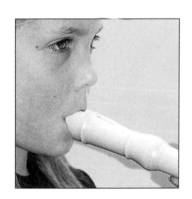

Wrong

Right

Tip: Take care to dry your mouth before you insert the recorder. The mouthpiece should stay as dry as possible.

Playing with the Head Joint

In order to get used to your instrument, we will only use the **head joint** of the recorder for the first few exercises, and not the whole recorder.

- Try creating different tones with just the head joint: low, high, loud and soft. Play these tones in different ways — some long, some short. Try experimenting with different methods of blowing.
- "Talk" while blowing into your recorder. Use syllables such as "doo", "day", "dah". You get the best mouth shape when saying "doo".
- Say long, even syllables ("doooooo") and short, truncated ones ("doo – doo – doo – doo").
- Try imitating everyday, familiar noises with the head of the recorder.

With all these exercises, take care to listen precisely to the sounds that you are creating with the head joint. This will help you to develop a feel for the instrument, as it probably still seems a little strange and unaccustomed.

Positioning Your Fingers

To play the recorder, bend your fingers slightly, but keep them relaxed.

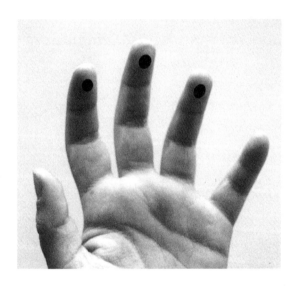

Cover the finger holes of the recorder with the pad, not the end, of each fingertip. It is very important to ensure that the holes are completely covered, because otherwise you won't produce the correct tones!

Take a look at the dots in the illustration to see which part of your fingers you should use in order to close the holes completely.

Each hole on the recorder is assigned a particular finger. The diagram below shows you which finger belongs to which hole.

Right Hand

Little finger

Ring finger

Middle finger

Index finger

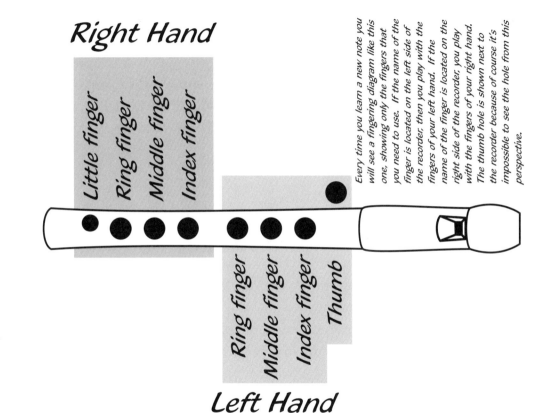

Ring finger

Middle finger

Index finger

Thumb

Left Hand

Every time you learn a new note you will see a fingering diagram like this one, showing only the fingers that you need to use. If the name of the finger is located on the left side of the recorder, then you play with the fingers of your left hand. If the name of the finger is located on the right side of the recorder, you play with the fingers of your right hand. The thumb hole is shown next to the recorder because of course it's impossible to see the hole from this perspective.

Your First "Proper" Note – G

In this book, small illustrations will show you how to play new notes. They will show you which holes should stay open (white circle) and which ones should be covered by your fingers (black circle).

Now it's time for your first note – G. You only need the fingers on your left hand for this note.

Remember the following when trying out a new note:

• The finger holes indicated must be covered completely.
• Take care during playing to hold the recorder safely with two hands.

Ring finger

Middle finger

Index finger

Thumb

The note G

14

- As far as possible, try to breathe in a controlled and even manner while blowing (imagine the air flowing from your mouth in a long, regular stream).

Now try experimenting with G in order to obtain a feel for your instrument. Play it long and short or loud and soft. Take care to produce an even sound and make sure no air flows past the recorder.

The Note A

Once you have mastered G, you can immediately try the next note: A.
To make an A, you only need the index finger, middle finger and thumb of your left hand.
Now try playing G and A one after the other, and then also the other way round, i.e. with A following G. Try this several times.

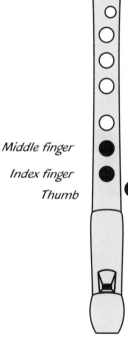

Middle finger
Index finger
Thumb

The note A

Notation

Stem

Hook or tail

Head

A note

Notation makes it possible for us to be able to write down the tones needed to play a tune. A note comprises a note head and a note stem. Sometimes a note also has a hook or a tail. So that we know which pitch a note has, the note is written down in a system of notation (i.e. "notated".) A notation system consists of five lines. We call these five lines a staff or stave.

A staff with notes:

Notes can be written on the lines and also in the spaces in between – the most important aspect is always the head of the note. The higher up the note head is located on the staff, the higher the note that is played. Notes are read from left to right (like letters of the alphabet).

Clefs

So that we know that these five lines represent a notation system, they are preceded by a **clef**, which is written right at the beginning of each staff. The clef indicates the position of a note.

In this book we'll use a G clef (otherwise known as treble clef or violin clef). The G clef gets its name from the fact that it shows the **note G**. **G** is written on the second line from the bottom and the inner spiral of this clef precisely encircles this line on the staff.

The **note A** can be found in the space that is located above the note G.

G clef
(treble or violin clef)

The note G

The note A

Quarter Notes (Crotchets)

First of all, let's try a little exercise. Just count evenly from 1 to 4 and clap your hands at the same time.

One, two, three, four, One, two, three, four, One, two, three, four, etc.

Next, we will replace every number you say out loud with a note.
These notes are called **quarter notes** or crotchets.
They have a black note head and a stem.

Quarter note

Now play a quarter note instead of a number, using the note G.
- Play so that all the notes are exactly the same length.
- If possible, play them without any pauses between them.
- Count from 1 to 4 in your head as you play.

Count: 1   2   3   4   1   2   3   4   1   2   etc.

dooooooodooooooodoooooooodoooooodooooooodooooooodooooooodooooooodooooooodoooooo
Play it like this!

Measure

To make it easier to keep track of where you are in a piece of music, the notes are arranged in groups. We call one such group a **measure** or **bar**. The measures of a musical composition are separated from each other by long vertical strokes — the **bar lines**. In our first tunes, we will use groups of four, which we then call **4/4 meter** or **4/4 time** (say "four-four meter" or "four-four time") because one measure comprises four quarter notes. The meter is indicated before the first note, right at the beginning of the staff, immediately after the clef.

Count: 1   2   3   4   1   2   3   4

Time/meter

Bar line

First Practice Runs

In this exercise you will only play **quarter notes** (one beat notes). Try counting in your head so that the notes are all the same length.

After the fourth note, you will see that there is a breathing pause. If you have run out of air and cannot continue playing, this is the spot at which to catch your breath again. In several tunes we will suggest breathing intervals to you, but try finding out yourself when you need to inhale.

Breathing symbol

Count: 1   2   3   4   1   2   3   4

The next exercise takes up two staffs. When you arrive at the end of the first staff, you simply continue playing at the start of the next one.

At the end, you can see one thick and one thin bar line. We call this the **final double bar**. It marks the end of the tune.

Final double bar

Half Notes (Minims)

Half note

We will now play a **half note** or **minim**. It looks almost exactly like the quarter note but it has a white note head. The half note is double the length of the quarter note. Count two beats to each note, instead of one.

This is how you play two half notes:
doooooooooooooooooodooooooooooooooooooooodoooooooooooooooooodooooooooooooooooooo

Count: 1   2   3   4   1   2   3   4

This exercise comprises quarter notes and half notes. Don't forget to count as you proceed, and take care not to shorten the half notes.

Take a breathing pause at the end of each bar in this exercise.

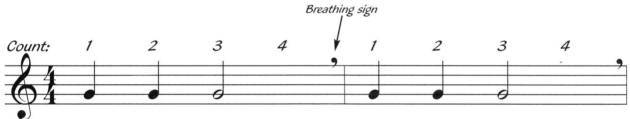

Jump Around

Your first real tune follows. It's called 'Jump Around'. You play it using the notes G and A.

Try to play the second row without a breathing pause.

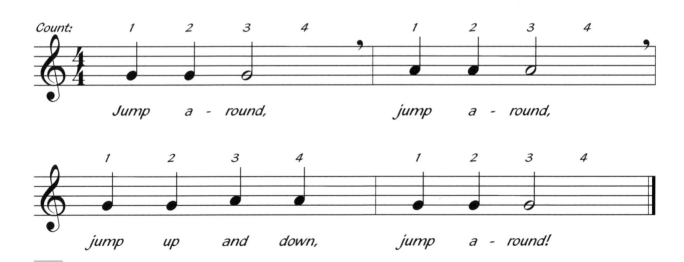

The Note B

The note B

The next note that you will learn is B. B is written on the middle line of the staff.

You have probably already noticed that the note stem, which is drawn on the left side of the note head, points downwards.

Index finger

Thumb

This is intentional and is not a mistake: all notes have stems that point downwards if they are located on or above the third staff line.

On the right, you can see which fingers to use to play B.

The note B

Play this exercise very slowly, because you will need to play the three notes that you already know, one after the other.

Sleep Tight

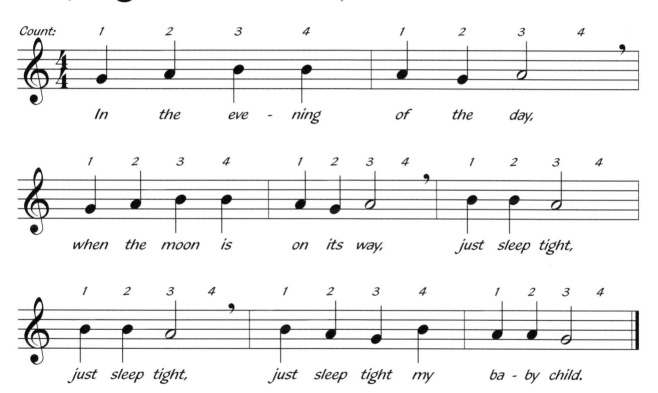

27

The Note C²

The note C²

And here is yet another new note, C in the second octave or C².

C² is written in the third space of the staff (counting from bottom to top).

The fingering diagram on the right shows you how to finger C². For this note, you need the middle finger and the thumb of your left hand.

Middle finger

Thumb

The note C²

The note C can be found in several places on the recorder. So that you can differentiate between the repeats, they are marked with numbers. The C^2 which you have just learned represents C in the second octave.
All other notes that you have learned so far (G, A and B) are notes with an " ^{1} ", i.e. G^1, A^1 and B^1. In order not to lose the overview on account of a multitude of numbers, I will omit the " ^{1} " and will only include the " ^{2} " on these notes.

In this exercise, you play all the notes that you know, i.e. G, A, B and C^2.

Count: 1   2   3   4   1   2   3   4   1   2   3   4   1   2   3   4

Dancing

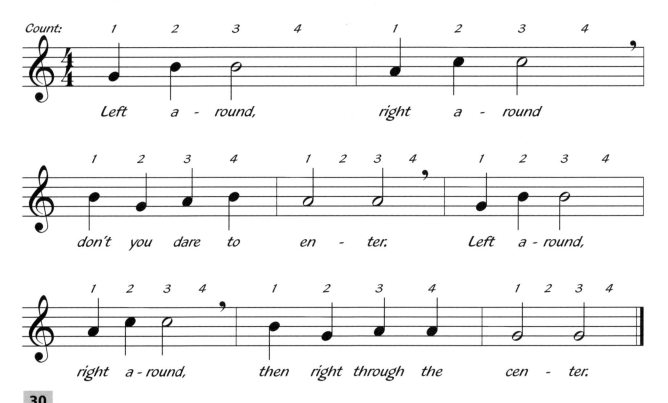

Dreams

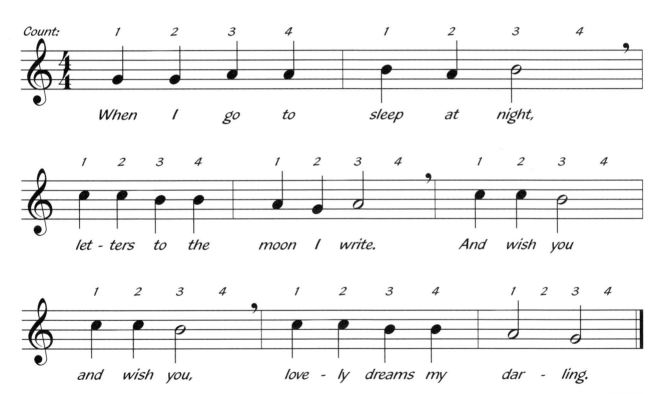

The Note D²

The note D²

The next piece requires another new note: D² (say "D in the second octave"). You will find it on the line above C², i.e. the fourth line from the bottom. Because it is located above the third line of the staff, its stem points downwards.

In order to play D², you only need one finger. Close the relevant finger hole with the middle finger of your left hand: I know it's not so easy because you still need to keep hold of the recorder.

Middle finger

The note D²

In this short exercise you will play a tune in which all the notes occur that you have learned so far, one after the other.

The next tune but one, "Dear Friends" is quite difficult. For this tune you will need to practice especially the notes B, C^2 and D^2. Here is some practice in doing that. You only need the middle finger, index finger and thumb of your left hand.

Once a Man

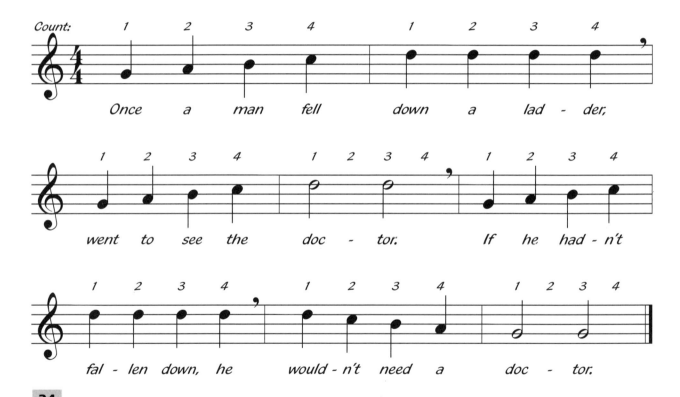

Dear Friends

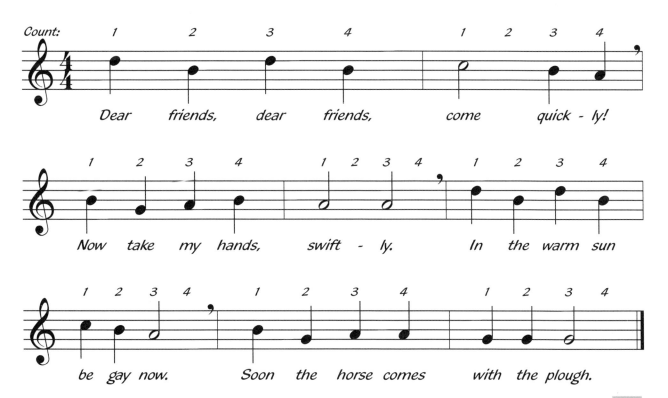

Count: 1 2 3 4 | 1 2 3 4

Dear friends, dear friends, come quick - ly!

1 2 3 4 | 1 2 3 4 | 1 2 3 4

Now take my hands, swift - ly. In the warm sun

1 2 3 4 | 1 2 3 4 | 1 2 3 4

be gay now. Soon the horse comes with the plough.

35

Take a Rest!

Half rest

In notation there are, of course, also symbols for times when you don't have to play anything: these are the rest symbols. The first of these symbols that you will learn is the **half rest** or minim rest.

The half rest is a short, very thick stroke that sits **on** the third staff line.
The half rest has exactly the same length as a half note. So, for the length of two beats, you play nothing at all.

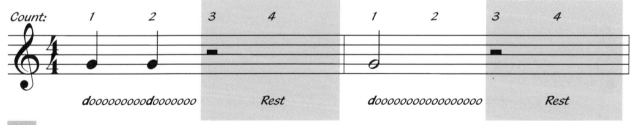

Count: 1   2   3   4   1   2   3   4

dooooooooodoooooooo   Rest   doooooooooooooooooo   Rest

When a rest symbol appears in the notation, you don't have to play anything but you should still stay "prepared". Leave the recorder in your mouth or at least keep it close to your mouth because after every rest you will have to continue playing at some point.
Besides, rests are ideal places for catching your breath ... try it in the next exercise:

Little Jack

This is your first "real" song and the notes for it are spread over this and the following page. Count along to the half rests to make sure they last as long as they're supposed to.

Count: 1 2 3 4   1 2 3 4   1 2 3 4

Lit - tle Jack,   with his pack,   wan - dered down the

1 2 3 4   1 2 3 4   1 2 3 4

rail - road track.   Lit - tle Jack,   stick and hat,

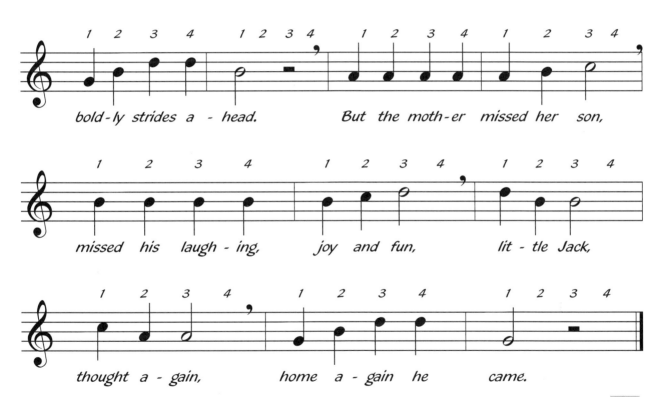

bold-ly strides a - head.   But the moth-er missed her son,

missed his laugh - ing,   joy and fun,   lit - tle Jack,

thought a - gain,   home a - gain he   came.

39

Rest Now

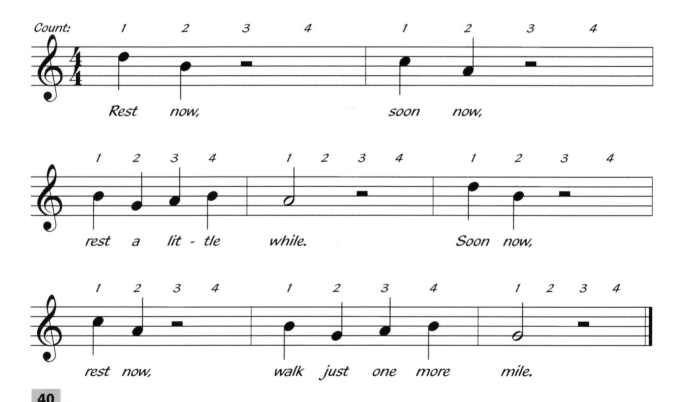

Go, Tell Aunt Rhody

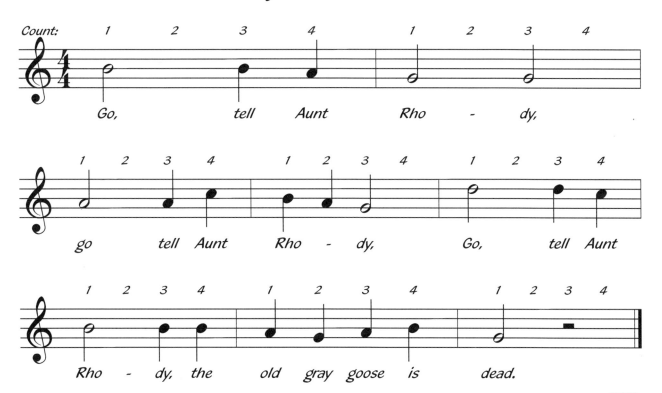

The Note F

The note F

The note F is located in the first space of the staff, directly below G.

Because it is located below the third line of the staff, F has a stem that points upwards.

Little Finger
Ring finger
Index finger

Ring finger
Middle finger
Index finger
Thumb

See the illustration on the right for the correct fingering position. This fingering is quite difficult but it produces a good sound.

The note F

Color this picture!

Here are two exercises for our new note F.

Practice them very slowly until you have got used to fingering with your right hand.

Exercise 1

Exercise 2

Darling

A Short Rest

Quarter rest

For the next tune you need to learn a new type of rest - the **quarter rest** or crotchet rest.
It has exactly the same length as a quarter note.
Because of its unusual shape, the quarter rest is very easy to recognize.

The same number of quarter rests and quarter notes (i.e. four) fit into a 4/4 meter.

Here are two short exercises with lots of quarter rests.

The rests should be neither too long nor too short. This is why you should always count along.

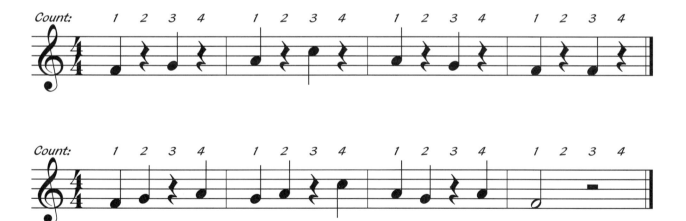

When the Saints
Go Marchin' In

There's only one quarter rest in the next tune, but there are many half rests.

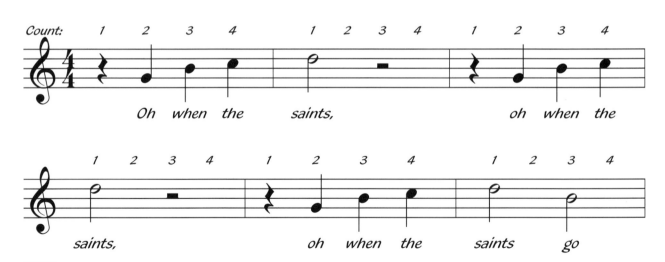

Count: 1   2   3   4   1   2   3   4   1   2   3   4

Oh when the   saints,   oh when the

1   2   3   4   1   2   3   4   1   2   3   4

saints,   oh when the   saints   go

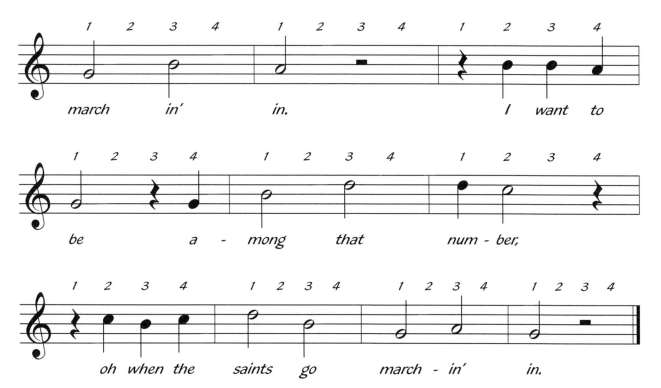

49

Chinese Dance

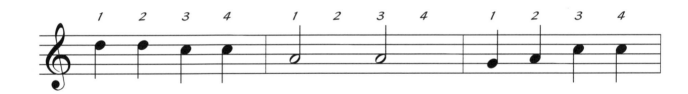

The Note E

The note E

The next note is called E.

It is located on the bottom line of the staff, i.e. directly below F.

The fingering diagram on the right shows you how to correctly finger E.

Middle finger

Index finger

Ring finger
Middle finger
Index finger
Thumb

The note E

You have already learned 7 notes now.

Play all the notes in the next exercise, one after the other – up and down the scale once.

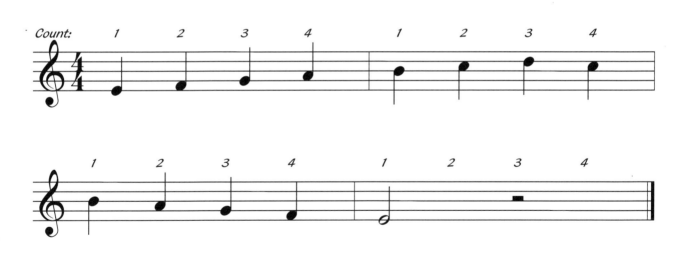

Easy

This tune contains all the notes you have learned so far.

Count: 1 2 3 4 | 1 2 3 4 | 1 2 3 4 | 1 2 3 4

E, G, F, A, B, A and C.

1 2 3 4 | 1 2 3 4 | 1 2 3 4 | 1 2 3 4

This is ea - sy can't you see?

Little Pussy

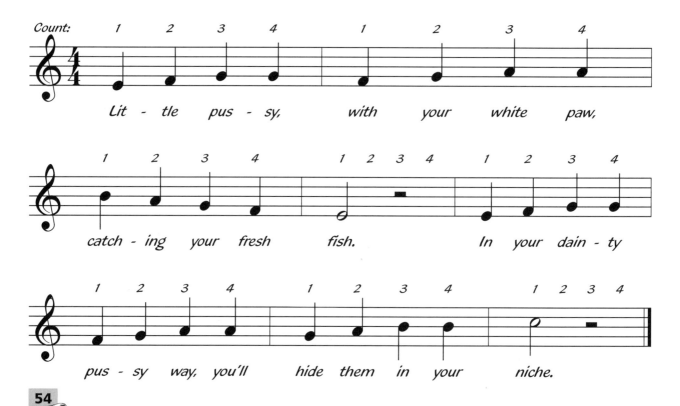

The Note D

The note D

The note D is "stuck" just below the lowest line of the staff.

Ring finger
Middle finger
Index finger

Ring finger
Middle finger
Index finger
Thumb

To play D you need almost all your fingers. All but one of the holes are covered.

The note D

In this exercise you basically only need to pay attention to your right hand. The fingers of your left hand always stay on their holes. Only the fingers of your right hand have to be changed for each note.

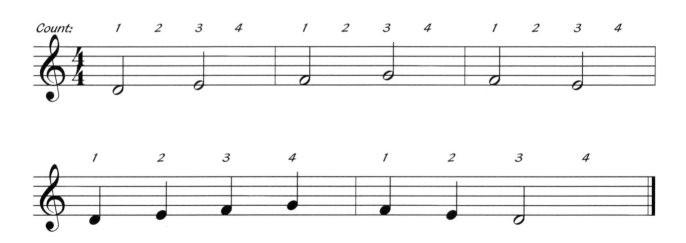

Higher and Higher

The Lowest Note: C

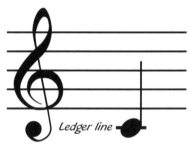

Ledger line

The note C

This is the lowest note that you can play.

To play C you need to cover up all the finger holes on your recorder.

In our system of notation, C lies below D. Since D is already located below the bottom line on the staff, an additional notation line has to be added for C. So that you can tell it from the "normal" 5 staff lines, this line is reduced so that it is only just slightly longer than the note to which it refers. Lines of the staff that have been shortened in this way are called **ledger lines**.

Little Finger

Ring finger

Middle finger

Index finger

Ring finger

Middle finger

Index finger

Thumb

The note C

We have now been through all the notes that you need for the tunes in this book. Now play them all, one after the other. Take care to ensure that all finger holes are completely covered.

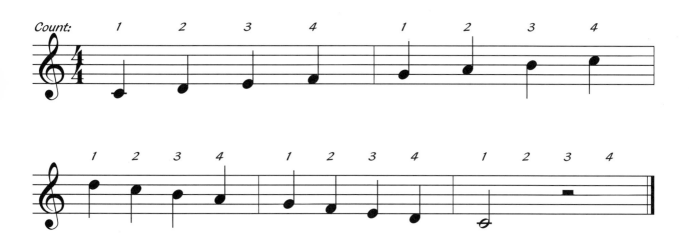

For the next tune you need lots of low notes in particular.

London Bridge Is Falling Down

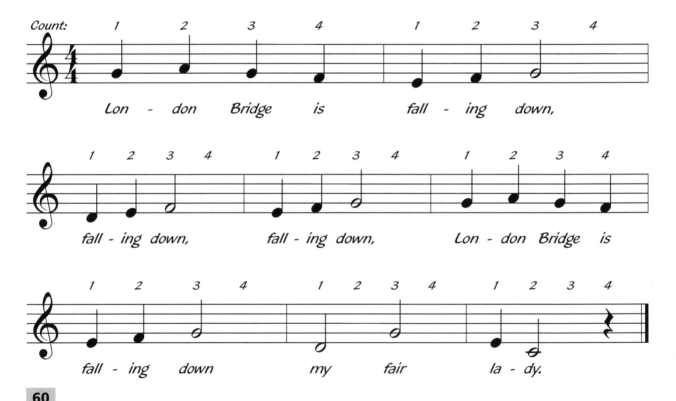

Color this
picture!

Twinkle, Twinkle, Little Star

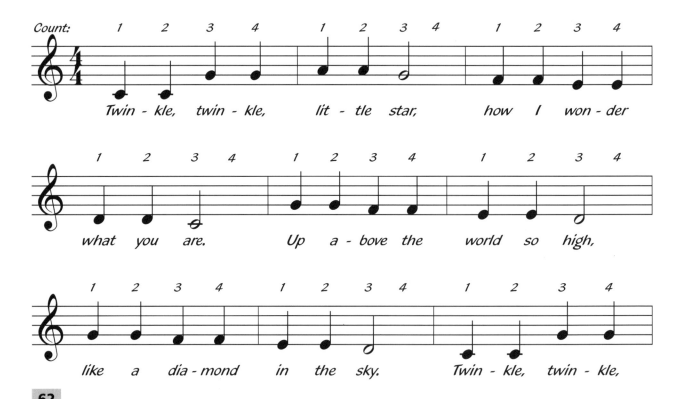

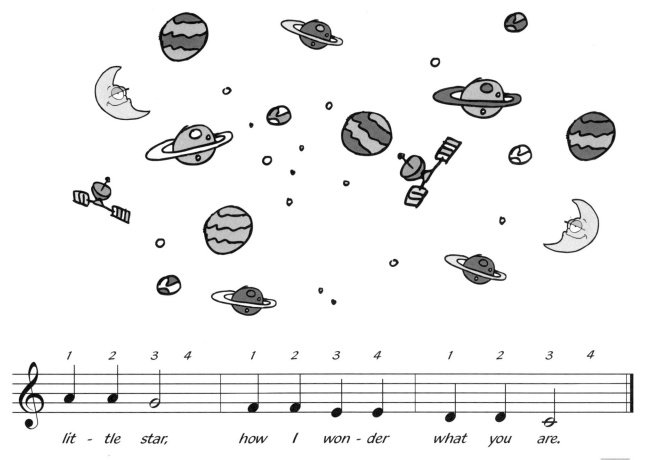

Whole Notes and Whole Rests

Whole note

At the end of a tune we usually need a **whole note** (semibreve).
It fills a complete measure by itself and lasts for four beats.

Whole notes have a white, unfilled note head and no stem.

As with the quarter note and the half note, there is also a rest equivalent to a whole note: the **whole rest** (or semibreve rest), but you rarely encounter this in tunes.

The **whole rest** "hangs" from the fourth staff line and has exactly the same length as a whole note (i.e. four beats).

The whole rest is commonly written in the middle of a measure.

Whole rest

Careful! The whole rest looks almost exactly like the half rest, but there is a small difference between the two: The whole rest "hangs" below the fourth staff line, whereas the half rest "sits" on the third staff line. Compare both rests in the following illustration.

Count: 1   2   3   4   1   2   3   4   1   2   3   4   1   2   3   4

Whole rest   Half rest

All My Ducks

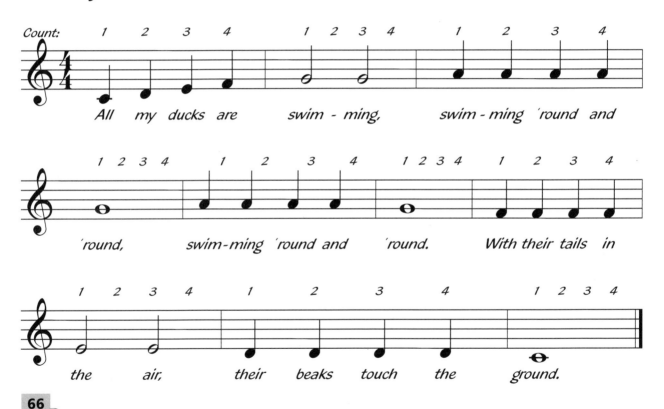

Sleep, Baby, Sleep

Count: 1 2 3 4 | 1 2 3 4 | 1 2 3 4

Sleep, ba - by, sleep. Your fa - ther tends the

1 2 3 4 | 1 2 3 4 | 1 2 3 4

sheep. Your moth - er shakes the dream - land tree, down

1 2 3 4 | 1 2 3 4 | 1 2 3 4 | 1 2

falls a lit - tle dream for thee. Sleep, ba - by, sleep.

The Upbeat

If you look at the first and last measures in the next tune, you will notice that several notes are missing from each. The first measure contains only one quarter note instead of four.

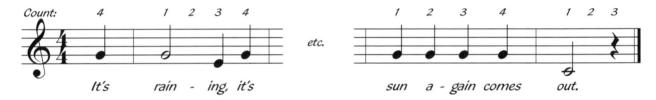

We call an incomplete measure at the start of a tune the **upbeat**. You will find the notes that are missing in the first measure in the final one. In tunes that contain an upbeat we find that the first and last measures combine to form a "whole" measure.

It's really easy to play an upbeat: You play the measure quite normally in your head (1 2 3 4) but don't start to play until you get to the first note. In this case, for example, you start playing at "4" with the note C. Easy, isn't it?

It's Raining

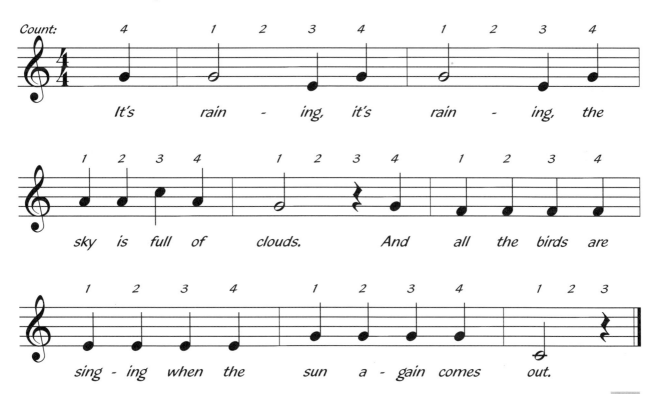

The Moon

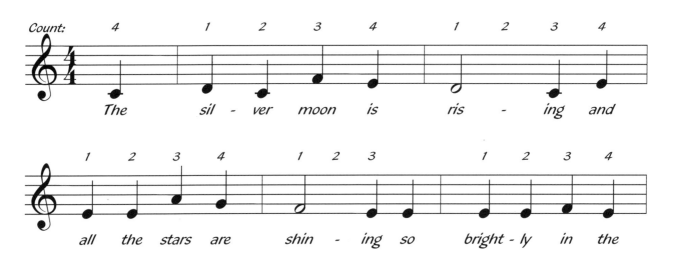

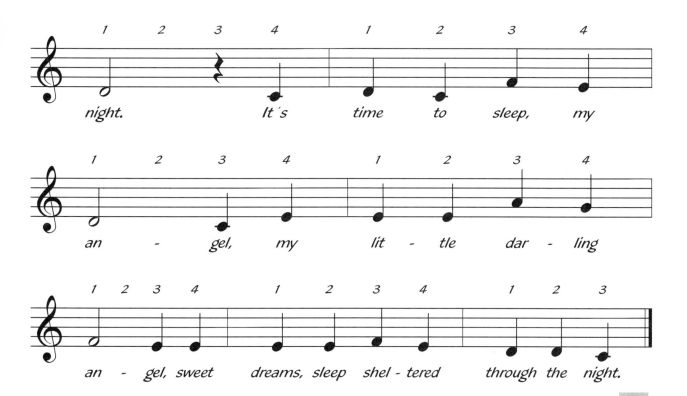

71

Eighth Notes

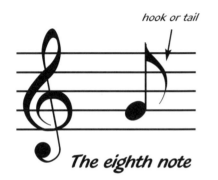

hook or tail

The eighth note

The last note that you will need in this book is an **eighth note** or **quaver**. It lasts exactly half as long as the quarter note. In other words, two eighth notes equal one quarter note.
The eighth note is easy to recognize by its hook or tail.

When two or more eighth notes are located next to each other, they are usually joined by a **cross bar**.

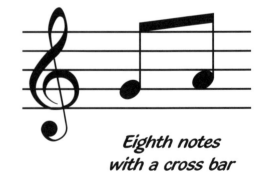

**Eighth notes
with a cross bar**

You need to play eighth notes exactly twice as fast as quarter notes.

To play them evenly, count as follows:

1 and 2 and 3 and 4 and

You play an eighth note on every number and also on each "and".

Count: 1 and 2 and 3 and 4 and   1 and 2 and 3 and 4 and

In this exercise you start playing slowly, increase your speed and then decrease it again.

All the notes that you know occur: Whole notes, half notes, quarter notes and eighth notes. Take care to play evenly and not to change speed.

This Old Man

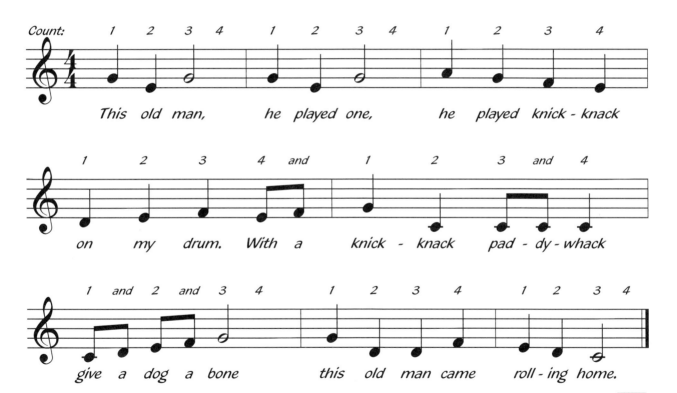

Baa, Baa, Black Sheep

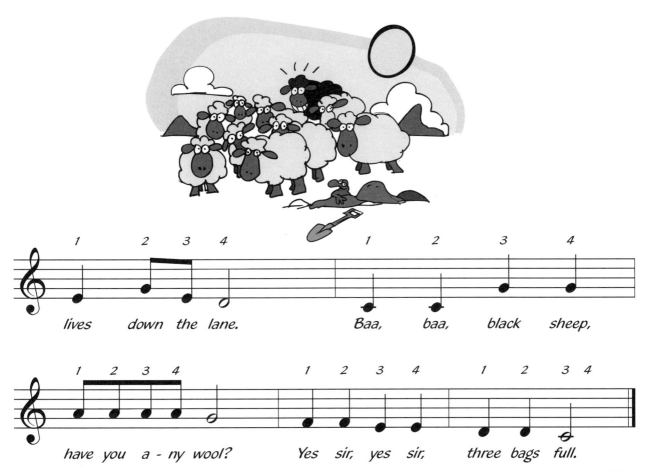

Teddy Bear

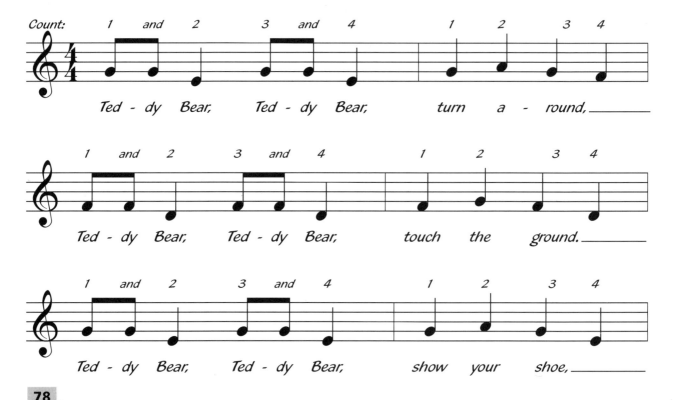

Eighth Rests

Eighth rest

Of course there is a rest that has exactly the same length as an eighth note: the **eighth rest** (or quaver rest).

Even if several eighth rests are located next to each other, they are not joined up with ties.

Count eighth rests exactly the same way as you count eighth notes, i.e. "1 and 2 and 3 and 4 and".

A Little Donkey

Three-four Meter

All the tunes that you have learned so far have been in 4/4 meter or 4/4 time (say it as "four-four meter" or "four-four time"), so you always counted **1 2 3 4.** But there are also other types of meter, such as **3/4 meter** (say it as "three-four meter").

Only three quarter notes fit into a bar with 3/4 meter. So you count

123 123 123 123 etc.

Just like in 4/4 meter, 3/4 meter is also indicated at the start of the first line of the staff so that the musician knows what to play.

Notes in 3/4 meter look like this:

So that you get used to 3/4 meter, count out loud:

123 123 123 123 123 123 123 123 etc.

and try emphasizing the number 1 a little.

After that, play the next exercise and count along in your head:

My Hat It Has Three Corners

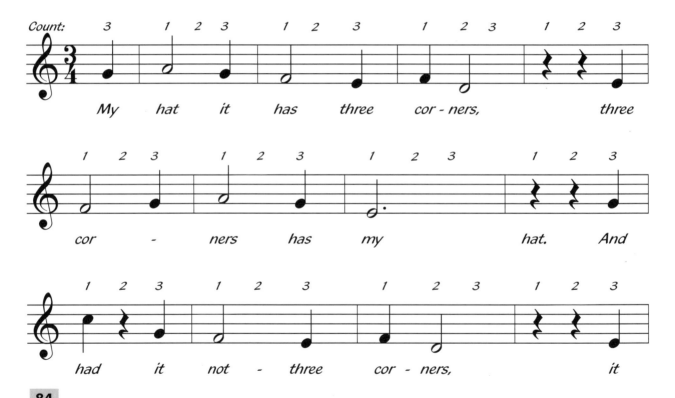

would   *not*   *be*   *my*   *hat.*

There's a Hole in the Bucket

Repeat Signs

Up till now, you have played all the tunes once through, from beginning to end. But in many tunes some measures or even larger sections are played twice. To save writing so many notes, musicians developed an "abbreviation system" early on for these double sections, i.e. **repeat signs**.

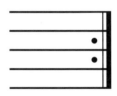

Repeat sign

The most important is the simple **repeat sign**. It looks like a final double bar with two small dots.

If you see this symbol at the end of a tune, you simply "jump" back to the beginning and play everything again from that point onwards.

But there are also tunes in which only a certain section is repeated. Then you will see an inverted repeat sign at the beginning of this section and a normal repeat sign at the end of this section.

These measures are played twice.

Often, you will see so-called *"boxes"*. They look like this:

First of all you play these measures.

Then you start again here.

And then carry on here.

1.

2.

Here, the first time, you play as far as the repeat sign at the end of the first box. When you come to play the repeat you omit the first box and continue playing from the second box.

Lavender's Blue

Count: 1 2 3   1 2 and 3 and   1 2 3   1 2 3

La - ven - der's   blue, dil - ly, dil - ly,   La - ven - der's   green;
Who told you   so,   dil - ly, dil - ly,   who told you   so?

1. 1 2 3   1 2 and 3 and   1 2 3   1 2 3

when I am King, dil - ly, dil - ly,   you shall be   queen.

2. 1 2 3   1 2 and 3 and   1 2 3   1 2 3

'Twas mine own heart, dil - ly, dil - ly,   that told me   so.

90

Talk to Me

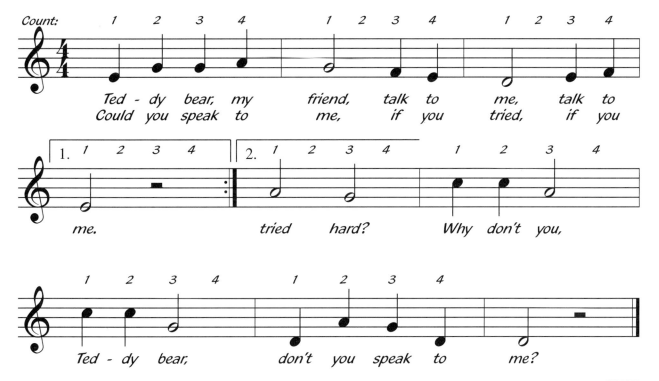

Count: 1 2 3 4   1 2 3 4   1 2 3 4

Ted - dy bear, my   friend, talk to   me, talk to
Could you speak to   me, if you   tried, if you

1. 1 2 3 4   2. 1 2 3 4   1 2 3 4

me.   tried hard?   Why don't you,

1 2 3 4   1 2 3 4

Ted - dy bear,   don't you speak to me?

Dotted Notes

If there is a dot behind a note, the note lasts half as long again as it did before:

Dotted quarter note

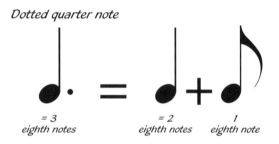

A **dotted quarter note** or **crotchet** is a combination of a quarter note and an eighth note in length (i.e. the length of three eighth notes).

Dotted half note

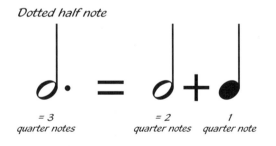

A **dotted half note** or **dotted minim** is a combination of a half note and a quarter note (i.e. the length of three quarter notes).

Rests can also be lengthened by a dot. Just like notes, they are extended by half.

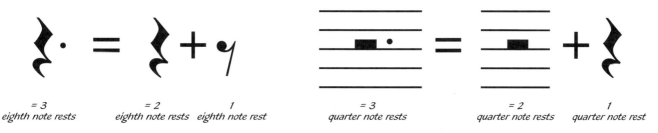

= 3
eighth note rests

= 2
eighth note rests

1
eighth note rest

= 3
quarter note rests

= 2
quarter note rests

1
quarter note rest

So that you don't get confused while counting, I have inserted numbers above the notes of all the difficult spots with dotted notes. We then have:

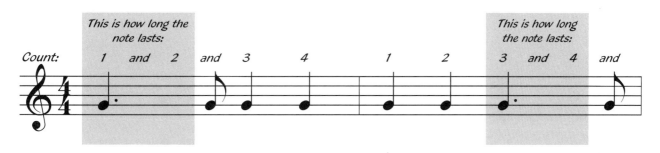

Goodnight Ladies

Count: 1 2 3 4 1 2 3 4 1 2 3 4 1 2 3 4

Good - night,   La - dies!   Good - night,   La - dies!

1 2 3 4 1 2 3 4 1 and 2 3 4

Good - night,   La - dies,   we're   go - ing to   leave   you

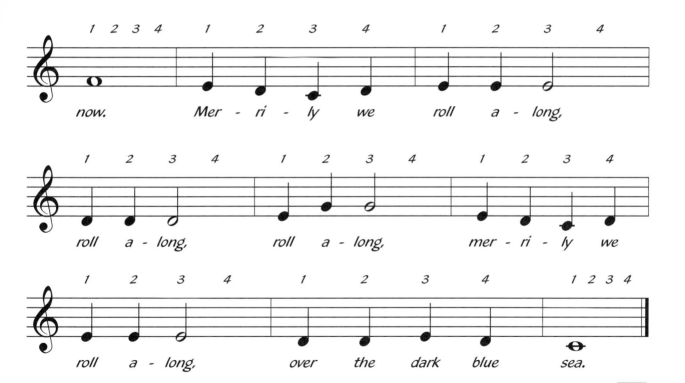

Oh, Susanna

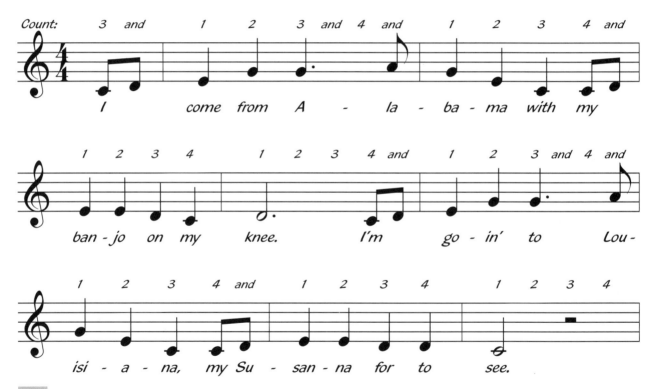

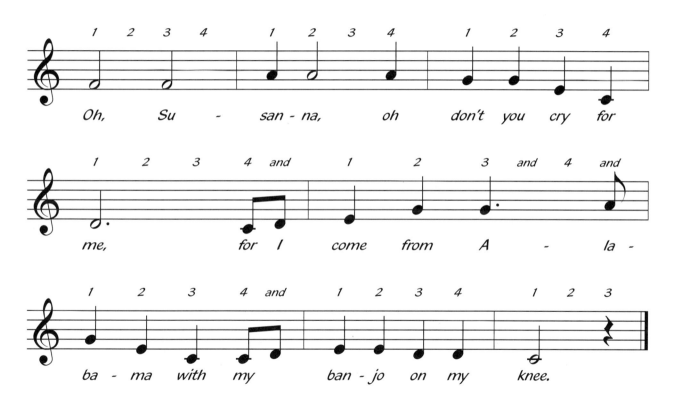

Brahms' Lullaby

Attention: This tune is in 3/4 meter.
So only count up to 3.

Count: 3   and   1   and   2   and   3   1   2   3   and

Lull - a - by,   and   good   night,   with

1   2   and 3   and   1   2   3   and   1   2   3   and

pink   ro -   ses   be - dight,   with   li - lies   o - ver-

Ties

Two notes of the **same pitch** are sometimes connected to each other by a **tie**. That means that these two notes are counted together and are played as a single note. The second note is not played again.

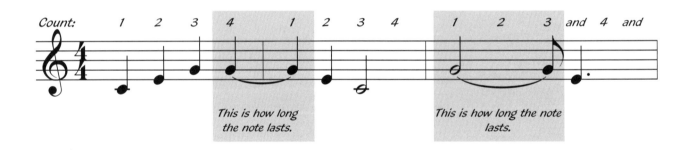

This is how long the note lasts.

This is how long the note lasts.

You can try it out straight away in the tune "Cheeky Monster".

The Cheeky Monster

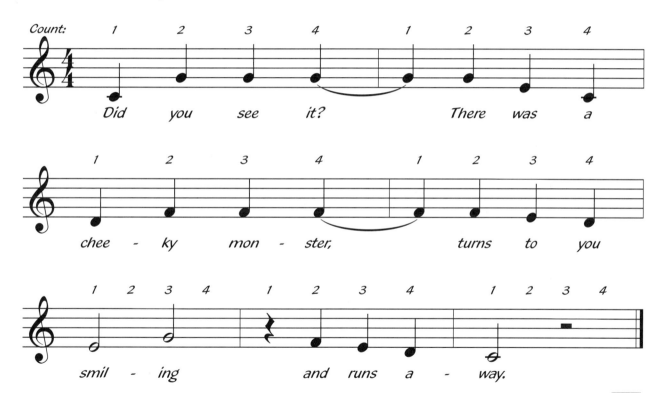

Legato and Staccato

It is possible to play notes on the recorder, one after the other, in very different ways.

Up till now you have played each note with a "doo" sound.

Legato is when two or more notes of different pitch are connected with each other by a slur. In this case, you play the first note with "doo" and make it last over the length of the other notes under the slur. In other words, don't repeat "doo" for each note - just open and close the finger holes for the other notes under the slur while still sounding the "doo" for the first note.

Staccato *is what is meant when you see dots above or below the note heads. In this case, the notes are separated clearly from each other and there is even a gap between them. They are all played a little shorter than indicated by the notes.*

Try alternating between staccato and legato in this exercise:

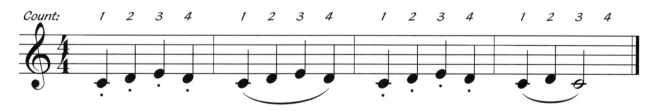

Nick, the Little Dragon

The Cuckoo and the Donkey

In this tune, play the first part staccato (doo, doo, doo).
After that you will encounter two short legato slurs (dooo-ooo). Where the syllables of a word are spread over two notes, the notes are played legato.
Play the last line like you did in all previous tunes (doodoodoo).

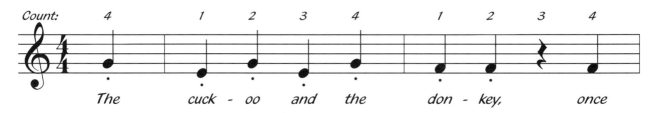

Count: 4   1   2   3   4   1   2   3   4

The   cuck - oo and the   don - key,   once

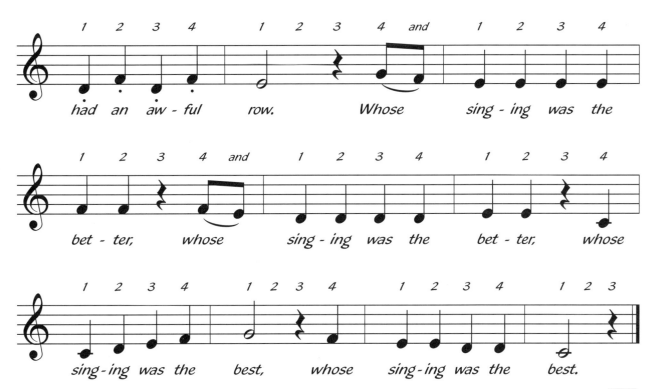

Appendix

Congratulations!
If you have managed to get this far, you can already play a recorder. Here are a few tips for the future.

A Word on Practicing

No musician likes to practice but there are a few simple tricks in order to make practicing as interesting and pleasant as possible.

1. Never practice when you don't feel like it! If you have to force yourself to practice, then it would be better not to start. If you notice while practicing that your mind is wandering elsewhere, stop practicing immediately.
2. It's better to practice daily for 20 minutes than to do nothing for two weeks and then three hours in a row. It's more important to practice regularly than at length.
3. If your hands become painful while playing, or if you notice pain in your body, stop immediately because your posture is probably cramped. Playing the recorder properly should never be painful.

Care of Your Recorder

For years of lasting enjoyment with your recorder, you should give it some basic care.

• After each session, take the instrument apart and wipe it off with a soft cloth. Then leave the recorder outside its case to dry. Wooden recorders cannot tolerate very high temperatures, direct sunshine or dry air. In order to protect your recorder from cracks, always store it in separate parts and put the parts together shortly before playing.

• In addition to this basic care, recorders made of wood should be regularly oiled in order to protect them from humidity. In normal use this is generally only necessary every few weeks. Please use only oil recommended to you for your recorder by your music store. Also ask which parts of your recorder should be oiled (not all recorders are oiled in the same way).

Fingering Chart

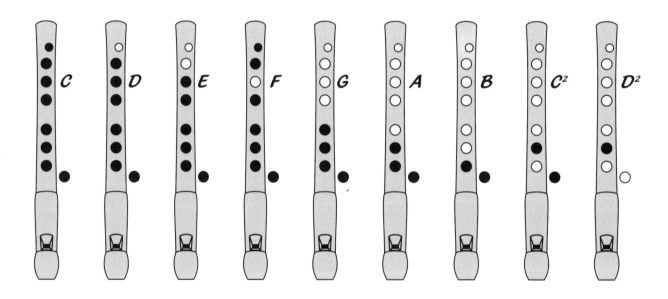

Alphabetical List of Tunes

Voggy's Recorder Songbook

In this book we have put
together well in excess of 40 of
the nicest and best-loved folk tunes
and children's rhymes for the soprano (descant)
recorder in C.

All tunes have been arranged for beginners and – where
necessary – simplified with care. This makes this Recorder Songbook not
only the ideal supplement to Voggy's Recorder Book; it is also excellent for use
with every other tutor book or as a collection of melodies.

DIN A5 Landscape format, 112 pages

Further information: www.voggenreiter.de